NATIONAL FOOTBALL LEAGUE
MEGASTARS

NFL

by **James Preller**

MS. E. RODRIGUEZ

SCHOLASTIC INC.

New York   Toronto   London   Auckland   Sydney
Mexico City   New Delhi   Hong Kong   Buenos Aires

ISBN 0-439-69177-X

Published by Scholastic Inc.
SCHOLASTIC and associated logos are trademarks and/or registered trademarks of Scholastic Inc.

12 11 10 9 8 7 6 5 4 3   4 5 6 7 8/0

Designed by Michael Malone
Printed in the U.S.A.
First printing, September 2004

You know what is really cool about NFL football?

It is a team game—maybe the ultimate team game. There are eleven players to a side, and each man must execute his job perfectly in order for the team to succeed. If an offensive lineman misses a block, the quarterback is in trouble. If the quarterback throws the ball too high, not even the most acrobatic receiver will be able to catch it. Everyone has a role—a purpose. But some players are so talented and competitive that they stand out above all others. When the game is on the line, they want the ball. They make big plays. They thrive on pressure. As a result, their teammates rally around them. They are leaders—in every sense of the word. And this book is devoted to them.

DERRICK
BROOKS

LINEBACKER
TAMPA BAY
BUCCANEERS

BORN: 4/18/1973
HEIGHT: 6-0
WEIGHT: 235
COLLEGE: FLORIDA STATE

[They couldn't weigh my heart, and I feel there's no **bigger heart** than mine.]

NO DOUBT

Derrick Brooks has always believed in himself, even when others have not. After college, some people thought he was too small to play in the NFL, but Derrick would not listen. One team wanted him to play defensive back. They invited him to work out for their scouts and coaches. Derrick said, "Thanks, but no thanks." He was determined to play the position he loved: linebacker. Guess what happened? The Tampa Bay Buccaneers gave Derrick a shot. And he did not let them down. With his unique combination of speed and strength, Derrick presents quite a challenge to opponents. He can cover even the fastest receivers, and he can challenge the toughest offensive linemen. In other words, he can do it all! Derrick led the Bucs to a Super Bowl title in 2002 and was named NFL Defensive Player of the Year! No one is doubting him now.

DID YOU KNOW? TO ENCOURAGE KIDS TO WORK HARD IN SCHOOL, DERRICK SPONSORS A PROGRAM KNOWN AS "BROOKS BUNCH." TO BE IN THE PROGRAM, STUDENTS HAVE TO MAINTAIN GOOD GRADES AND STAY OUT OF TROUBLE.

BROOKS BY THE NUMBERS
2003 SEASON ▶ GAMES: 16 • TACKLES: 71 • ASSISTS: 30 • SACKS: 1 • INTERCEPTIONS: 2

DAVID
CARR

QUARTERBACK
HOUSTON TEXANS

BORN: 7/21/1979
HEIGHT: 6-3
WEIGHT: 230
COLLEGE: FRESNO STATE

[I've always enjoyed making throws with a little **flair.** I like being different.]

ON THE RISE

As far as David Carr is concerned, no game is ever out of reach. With just two NFL seasons under his belt, the Texans' quarterback has already established a reputation for toughness and poise that would make many more-experienced players envious. His "never say die" approach to the game has helped make Houston competitive entering the franchise's third year of existence. It's also made David one of the more exciting players to watch. With a cannon for a right arm and an uncanny ability to read defenses, David is making good on the promise of his college career. As a senior at Fresno State he led the nation in both passing yards and touchdown passes. He also won the Johnny Unitas Award as the top quarterback in college football. Unitas, of course, was one of the NFL's all-time greats. David Carr is just getting warmed up.

DID YOU KNOW?
ONE OF THE REASONS HOUSTON MADE DAVID THE FIRST PICK IN THE 2002 NFL DRAFT WAS HIS STRENGTH. HE CAN BENCH-PRESS 390 POUNDS!

CARR BY THE NUMBERS
2003 SEASON ▶ GAMES: 12 • PASSING ATTEMPTS: 295 • COMPLETIONS: 167 • TDS: 9 • YARDS: 2,013

DAUNTE
CULPEPPER

© David STluka/NFL Photos

**QUARTERBACK
MINNESOTA VIKINGS**

BORN: 1/28/1977
HEIGHT: 6-4
WEIGHT: 260
COLLEGE: CENTRAL FLORIDA

[I can take a **pounding.** But I can give a pounding, too.]

THE INCREDIBLE HULK

All you have to do is look at Daunte Culpepper and you will realize he is no ordinary quarterback. First of all, he is absolutely huge. At six-feet-four, 260 pounds, Daunte is the biggest quarterback in the NFL. In fact, he is beefier than any of the Vikings' three starting linebackers! But there is more to Daunte than mere bulk. There is speed, for example. He runs the 40-yard dash in 4.42 seconds, which is faster than many fullbacks. There is strength, too. Daunte can bench-press 400 pounds! No wonder he has been known to uncork passes of 75 yards or more. Daunte is one of the NFL's most exciting quarterbacks. With every snap of the ball, there is the potential for something amazing to happen. Will Daunte run? Will he pass? Sometimes even he is not sure. That is what makes him so dangerous. And so much fun to watch!

DID YOU KNOW? DAUNTE IS ALSO A VERY TALENTED BASEBALL PLAYER. HE WAS SELECTED BY THE NEW YORK YANKEES IN THE 1995 MAJOR LEAGUE DRAFT, BUT CHOSE TO PLAY FOOTBALL INSTEAD. IT SEEMS LIKE HE MADE THE RIGHT DECISION.

**CULPEPPER BY THE NUMBERS
2003** SEASON ▶ GAMES: 14 • PASSING ATTEMPTS: 454 • COMPLETIONS: 295 • TDS: 25 • YARDS: 3,479

JAKE
DELHOMME

Top: © Kevin Terrell/NFL Photos. Bottom: © Joseph V. Labolito/NFL Photos

QUARTERBACK
CAROLINA PANTHERS

BORN: 1/10/1975
HEIGHT: 6-2
WEIGHT: 215
COLLEGE: LOUISIANA-LAFAYETTE

[Sometimes I have to **pinch myself** to believe I'm actually here.]

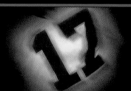

NEVER GIVE UP

There was a time when the NFL's Europe League was considered a consolation prize. You played there only if you were not good enough to cut it in the big time. That perception is changing—especially for quarterbacks. Kurt Warner and Brad Johnson are both graduates of NFL Europe, and both have Super Bowl rings. Now there is Jake Delhomme, the hard-throwing, fast-talking QB from Louisiana. Jake spent the better part of six years sitting on the bench. He did not get to play much. That's why he spent two seasons in Europe—so that he could stay sharp and continue to improve. Jake is an exciting, athletic quarterback who does not mind taking chances. He throws passes into the thickest of coverage. Somehow, he completes most of them. Thanks to his leadership and talent, the Panthers reached the Super Bowl in January of 2004. They did not win, but if Jake has anything to say about it, the Panthers will be back soon!

DID YOU KNOW?
JAKE LOVES HORSES. IN FACT, HE'S A PARTNER IN A THOROUGHBRED HORSE RACING BUSINESS.

DELHOMME BY THE NUMBERS
2003 SEASON ▶ GAMES: 16 • PASSING ATTEMPTS: 449 • COMPLETIONS: 266 • TDS: 19 • YARDS: 3,219

AHMAN
GREEN

RUNNING BACK
GREEN BAY PACKERS

BORN: 2/16/1977
HEIGHT: 6-0
WEIGHT: 217
COLLEGE: NEBRASKA

[If I happen to **break a record,** so be it. But it's not really important to me.]

IN THE FOOTSTEPS OF A LEGEND

Before every game Ahman Green dims the lights and draws the blinds in his living room. Then he turns on the TV and watches videotaped highlights of his hero, the late Walter Payton, one of football's all-time greatest running backs. Ahman says that watching Payton helps get him in the mood to play football, and to perform at the highest level possible. The strategy seems to be working. Like his idol, Ahman is an explosive and versatile player. Not only can he run with the ball, but he can catch it, too. Ahman has been the team's leading rusher for the past four seasons. In 2003 he led the NFC with 1,883 yards. He has also been one of the league's most dangerous receivers. And if he does not have the ball, that's okay. Ahman, who has the tree-trunk legs of an offensive lineman, is perfectly content to block for his teammates. He will do anything to help the Packers win!

DID YOU KNOW? AHMAN UNDERSTANDS THE VALUE OF GETTING AN EDUCATION. HE WAS A TWO-TIME ACADEMIC ALL-STATE SELECTION IN HIGH SCHOOL, AND EARNED A DEGREE IN GEOGRAPHY FROM THE UNIVERSITY OF NEBRASKA.

GREEN BY THE NUMBERS
2003 SEASON ▶ GAMES: 16 • RUSHING ATTEMPTS: 355 • YARDS: 1,833 • AVERAGE: 5.3 • TDS: 15

MATT
HASSELBECK

QUARTERBACK
SEATTLE SEAHAWKS

BORN: 9/25/1975
HEIGHT: 6-4
WEIGHT: 223
COLLEGE: BOSTON COLLEGE

[My job is **simple:** Get the ball out of my hands
and into the hands of a **great athlete.**]

OUT OF THE SHADOWS

It has taken a while for the spotlight to find Matt Hasselbeck. While growing up he looked up to his father, Don, who was a tight end in the NFL. When Matt followed in his dad's footsteps and became a professional football player, he found himself sitting on the bench in Green Bay, watching one of the game's greatest quarterbacks, Brett Favre. Matt learned a lot from Brett, but what he really wanted was a chance to play. That opportunity came in 2001, when he was traded to the Seattle Seahawks. Matt is now one of the league's top quarterbacks. In 2003 he threw 3,841 yards for a team record and led the Seahawks into the playoffs. Their opponent? The Green Bay Packers. That is right—Matt faced his old teammate, Brett Favre. And he had one of the best games of his career. Even though the Seahawks lost in overtime, Matt made it clear that he had arrived as an NFL quarterback.

DID YOU KNOW?
FOOTBALL REALLY IS A FAMILY AFFAIR FOR THE HASSELBECKS. MATT HAS TWO YOUNGER BROTHERS WHO ALSO PLAYED AT BOSTON COLLEGE.

HASSELBECK BY THE NUMBERS
2003 SEASON ▶ GAMES: 16 • PASSING ATTEMPTS: 513 • COMPLETIONS: 313 • TDS: 26 • YARDS: 3,841

TORRY
HOLT

WIDE RECEIVER
ST. LOUIS RAMS

BORN: 6/5/1976
HEIGHT: 6-0
WEIGHT: 190
COLLEGE: NORTH CAROLINA ST.

[I'm always looking for that *edge* to
put myself ahead of the game.]

SLEEPLESS IN ST. LOUIS

The night before a game is the worst for Torry Holt. Or the best. It all depends on how you look at it. Torry is a perfectionist. He works as hard as any player in the NFL to improve his game and perform at the highest level. For him, Sunday is test day, and he always expects to get an *A*. So Torry does not sleep well during football season, and he barely sleeps at all on Saturday nights. He tosses and turns. He runs plays over and over in his mind. When he does nod off, sometimes he will dream about football. But don't get the wrong idea. It is not that Torry is nervous or scared. He is just excited. For him, morning cannot come soon enough. All Torry wants to do is put on his uniform and play. And the more important the game, the more excited he gets. They do not call him "Big Game" for nothing. Since arriving in St. Louis in 1999, Torry has twice led the league in receiving yardage. Just imagine what he might do if he could get a little rest!

DID YOU KNOW? TORRY DEVOTES MUCH OF HIS TIME IN THE OFF-SEASON TO THE TORRY HOLT FOUNDATION, FOUNDED IN 1999 IN HONOR OF HIS MOTHER, WHO DIED OF CANCER AT THE AGE OF 43.

HOLT BY THE NUMBERS
2003 SEASON ▶ GAMES: 16 • RECEPTIONS: 117 • YARDS: 1,696 • AVERAGE:14.5 • TDS: 12

CURTIS
MARTIN

BORN: 5/1/1973
HEIGHT: 5-11
WEIGHT: 205
COLLEGE: PITTSBURGH

[I'm an **over-achiever.** I work as hard as I can, **every day**—even in practice.]

IRON MAN

For a guy who did not even play organized football until his senior year in high school, Curtis Martin has had quite a career. He's a late bloomer who continues to grow and improve, even after a decade in the NFL. What makes Curtis so special? Well, for one thing, he is remarkably consistent. Curtis has never failed to gain at least 1,000 yards in a season. He is one of only two players to crack the 1,000-yard mark in each of his first nine seasons. The other player is Barry Sanders, one of the greatest backs in NFL history. So that puts Curtis in pretty fast company. With a nose for finding the slimmest of openings and an ability to accelerate in the open field, Curtis presents all kinds of headaches for opponents. Although Curtis has been named the Jets' most valuable player three times, he is equally proud of another accomplishment: being voted the most inspirational player by his teammates. And that's happened three times!

DID YOU KNOW? CURTIS IS CONSIDERED ONE OF THE NFL'S MOST GENEROUS MEN. HE FREQUENTLY VISITS CHILDREN IN LOCAL HOSPITALS. HE HAS MADE SOME GOOD FRIENDS THIS WAY, AND SOMETIMES EVEN GIVES OUT HIS HOME PHONE NUMBER TO HIS YOUNG FANS.

MARTIN BY THE NUMBERS
2003 SEASON ▶ GAMES: 16 • RUSHING ATTEMPTS: 323 • YARDS: 1,308 • AVERAGE: 4.0 • TDS: 2

WILL
SHIELDS

OFFENSIVE LINEMAN
KANSAS CITY CHIEFS

HEIGHT: 6-3
WEIGHT: 315
BORN: 9/15/1971
COLLEGE: NEBRASKA

[If you can affect the lives of other people, that should be your **goal.**]

WHERE THERE'S A WILL, THERE'S A WAY

Let us start with the obvious. Will Shields is one of the biggest, strongest, and most accomplished players in the NFL. He is a mountain made of flesh and muscle, opening holes for the Chiefs' running backs and providing a giant shield for their quarterback. Offensive linemen are the quiet heroes of professional football. They toil in obscurity while others get the glory. But those who know football understand Will's value. He has been voted to the Pro Bowl nine times. Will also happens to have one of the biggest hearts in all of professional sports. He is a tireless worker off the field, devoting countless hours to charitable causes. The "Will to Succeed Foundation" includes programs that combat domestic violence and offer assistance to underprivileged families. It is no wonder that Will received the biggest honor of his career in January, 2004, when he won the Walter Payton Award as the NFL Man of the Year.

DID YOU KNOW? WILL IS A TRUE IRON MAN. SINCE JOINING THE NFL IN 1993, HE HAS NOT MISSED A SINGLE GAME. HIS STREAK OF 176 CONSECUTIVE GAMES PLAYED IS ONE OF THE LONGEST IN LEAGUE HISTORY!

SHIELDS BY THE NUMBERS
2003 SEASON ▶ WILL IS A KEY MEMBER OF AN OFFENSIVE LINE THAT ALLOWED ONLY 21 SACKS (SECOND FEWEST IN AFC).

MICHAEL
STRAHAN

© Larry French/NFL Photos

**DEFENSIVE END
NEW YORK GIANTS**

BORN: 11/21/1971
HEIGHT: 6-5
WEIGHT: 275
COLLEGE: TEXAS SOUTHERN

[When you tackle the quarterback, it's like
the **perfect moment** in life.]

THE SACK KING

Ask anyone who has ever met Michael Strahan. He is one of the nicest guys in the NFL. Off the field he is like a gentle giant—all smiles and handshakes and generosity. But do not mistake his goodwill for softness. And whatever you do, please...do not stand between Michael and the opposing quarterback. You are liable to get trampled! Something happens to Michael when the ball is snapped and the QB drops back to pass. It is like a switch is thrown and he becomes a guided missile. Although Michael is big and strong, he uses more than just power to wreak havoc on defense. He is also a smart player who knows exactly when to charge at the quarterback, and how to avoid blocks along the way. That combination of intelligence, desire, and talent helped earn Michael a place in the record books in 2001 when he broke the record for most sacks in a single season. Someday he will have a place in the Pro Football Hall of Fame, as well.

DID YOU KNOW? MICHAEL PLAYED ONLY ONE YEAR OF HIGH SCHOOL FOOTBALL. BECAUSE HIS FATHER WAS IN THE U.S. ARMY, THE FAMILY MOVED AROUND A LOT. MICHAEL SPENT MOST OF HIS TEENAGE YEARS IN GERMANY, WHERE HIS FATHER WAS STATIONED. AND IN GERMANY, *FOOTBALL* MEANS SOCCER!

**STRAHAN BY THE NUMBERS
2003** SEASON ▶ GAMES: 16 • TACKLES: 61 • ASSISTS: 15 • SACKS: 18.5

Top: © Jim Turner/NFL Photos. Bottom: © Al Messerschmidt/NFL Photos

LADAINIAN TOMLINSON

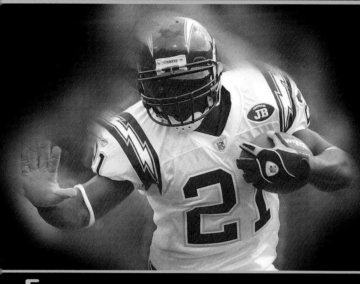

RUNNING BACK
SAN DIEGO CHARGERS

BORN: 6/23/1979
HEIGHT: 5-10
WEIGHT: 221
COLLEGE: TEXAS CHRISTIAN

[If you know what to do on the field, you can let
your **skills** and **ability** take over.]

STUDENT OF THE GAME

LaDainian Tomlinson makes it look so easy. He is one of the most explosive running backs in the NFL, as well as a sure-handed receiver. In fact, LaDainian led the league in total scrimmage yards in 2003. But do not be fooled. Although he is obviously a gifted athlete, LaDainian is also a man who believes in the value of preparation. Before his rookie year, LaDainian sought out two of football's all-time greatest running backs, Emmitt Smith and Marcus Allen, and asked for their advice. In training camp LaDainian not only memorized his playbook, but took notes every day, which helped him make an immediate impact in the NFL. He has rushed for more than 1,000 yards in each of his first three seasons. With lightning speed and moves that often leave defenders grasping at air, LaDainian is a record-breaking performer who seems destined to leave his mark on the game!

DID YOU KNOW?
IN 1999 LaDAINIAN RUSHED FOR 406 YARDS IN A GAME AGAINST TEXAS-EL PASO!
THAT'S AN NCAA DIVISION I-A RECORD.

TOMLINSON BY THE NUMBERS
2003 SEASON ▶ GAMES: 16 • RUSHING ATTEMPTS: 313 • YARDS: 1,645 • AVERAGE: 5.3 • TDS: 13

ADAM VINATIERI

KICKER
NEW ENGLAND PATRIOTS

HEIGHT: 6-0
WEIGHT: 202
BORN: 12/28/1972
COLLEGE: SOUTH DAKOTA STATE

[On any **field goal,** you have to put whatever came before it out of your mind. You have to **focus.**]

CLUTCH TIME

Have you ever wondered what it must be like to have a championship riding on your shoulders as time runs out? Can you imagine the pressure? The emotion? Well, if you are Adam Vinatieri, you don't have to wonder. You know exactly how it feels, because you have lived through it. Twice! In January of 2002, Adam led the "Cinderella" Patriots to a storybook finish when he kicked a 48-yard field goal as time expired. Most athletes dream of coming through in the clutch like that, but most never get a chance to prove they can do it. Adam did. Two years later he got another opportunity. This one was even more challenging. Adam missed his first two field goal attempts against the Carolina Panthers in Super Bowl XXXVIII. Would he have the confidence to hit the game-winner when he took the field with four seconds remaining and the score tied, 29-29? Yes! Adam calmly drilled the ball through the uprights to give the Pats their second championship in three years.

DID YOU KNOW? ADAM'S ANCESTOR FELIX WAS THE LEADER OF A BAND OF MUSICIANS THAT TRAVELED WITH GENERAL GEORGE CUSTER. FORTUNATELY, WHEN MARCHING INTO HIS FAMOUS LOSING BATTLE AGAINST NATIVE AMERICANS IN THE BLACK HILLS OF SOUTH DAKOTA, CUSTER LEFT THE MUSICIANS BEHIND.

VINATIERI BY THE NUMBERS
2003 SEASON ▶ GAMES: 16 • FG/ATTEMPTS: 25/34 • EXTRA POINTS/ATTEMPTS: 37/38 • TOTAL POINTS: 112

HINES
WARD

WIDE RECEIVER
PITTSBURGH STEELERS

BORN: 3/8/1976
HEIGHT: 6-0
WEIGHT: 200
COLLEGE: GEORGIA

[When I pull it down and go, **I'm gone.**]

NERVES OF STEEL

There is something you should know about Hines Ward. He is not like most wide receivers. You see, wideouts are usually among the smallest and most graceful players in the NFL. They use their speed and quickness to avoid contact with the giants of the game. It is a matter of survival. When you are only six feet tall and you run smack into a 240-pound linebacker, you're likely to get the worst of the deal. So you look for open space. Not Hines. He likes contact! You might even say that Hines has changed the way receivers are supposed to play. He can impact the game even when he does not have the ball in his hands. Of course, it lands there often enough. Hines has led the Steelers in receiving in each of the last four seasons and has played in three Pro Bowls as an AFC All-Star. If he were a little bit bigger, Hines would probably be a great offensive tackle. For now, he will settle for being one of the NFL's top receivers.

DID YOU KNOW?
HINES BEGAN HIS FOOTBALL CAREER AS A QUARTERBACK. IN FACT, HE WAS A HIGH SCHOOL ALL-AMERICAN AND ONE OF THE TOP PASSERS IN THE NATION!

WARD BY THE NUMBERS
2003 SEASON ▶ GAMES: 16 • RECEPTIONS: 95 • YARDS: 1,163 • AVERAGE: 12.2 • TDS: 10

ROY
WILLIAMS

SAFETY
DALLAS COWBOYS

BORN: 8/14/1980

HEIGHT: 6-0

WEIGHT: 235

COLLEGE: OKLAHOMA

[You've got to **attack.** If you stand there flat-footed, you're going to get **run over.**]

HAMMER TIME

Everyone likes Roy Williams. He is a pleasant, soft-spoken young man. On Sundays, however, something happens to Roy. When he puts on the uniform of the Dallas Cowboys, he is transformed into one of the toughest and most intimidating defenders in the NFL. Ask any wide receiver or running back unlucky enough to meet Roy in the open field. This is a guy who knows how to hit! No wonder they call him "Hammer." Not that Roy wants to hurt anyone. He is just a clean, strong player who patrols the secondary with intensity and seriousness. If you try to catch a pass in Roy's territory—watch out! You are going to pay a steep price. But Roy is more than just a big hitter. He is a gifted athlete with the speed to cover fleet-footed receivers, and the size to challenge even the biggest of running backs. As teammate Darren Woodson says, "There's not another safety in the league who can do what Roy does."

DID YOU KNOW?
ROY WON THE BRONKO NAGURSKI AWARD AS THE NATION'S TOP COLLEGE FOOTBALL DEFENSIVE PLAYER IN 2001.

WILLIAMS BY THE NUMBERS
2003 SEASON ▶ GAMES: 16 • TACKLES: 55 • ASSISTS: 17 • SACKS: 2 • INTERCEPTIONS: 2

Top & bottom: © James D. Smith/NFL Photos

JUST THE FACTS

NFL LEADERS

RUSHING YARDS

Year	Player	Yards
2003	Jamal Lewis	2,066
2002	Ricky Williams	1,853
2001	Priest Holmes	1,555
2000	Edgerrin James	1,709
1999	Edgerrin James	1,553
1998	Terrell Davis	2,008
1997	Barry Sanders	2,053
1996	Barry Sanders	1,553
1995	Emmitt Smith	1,773
1994	Barry Sanders	1,883
1993	Emmitt Smith	1,486
1992	Emmitt Smith	1,713
1991	Emmitt Smith	1,563
1990	Barry Sanders	1,304

PASSING YARDS

Year	Player	Yards
2003	Peyton Manning	4,267
2002	Rich Gannon	4,689
2001	Kurt Warner	4,830
2000	Peyton Manning	4,413
1999	Steve Beuerlein	4,436
1998	Brett Favre	4,212
1997	Jeff George	3,917
1996	Mark Brunell	4,367
1995	Brett Favre	4,413
1994	Drew Bledsoe	4,555
1993	John Elway	4,030
1992	Dan Marino	4,116
1991	Warren Moon	4,690
1990	Warren Moon	4,689

PASS RECEIVING YARDS

Year	Player	Yards
2003	Torry Holt	1,696
2002	Marvin Harrison	1,722
2001	David Boston	1,598
2000	Torry Holt	1,635
1999	Marvin Harrison	1,663
1998	Antonio Freeman	1,424
1997	Rob Moore	1,584
1996	Isaac Bruce	1,338
1995	Jerry Rice	1,848
1994	Jerry Rice	1,499
1993	Jerry Rice	1,503
1992	Sterling Sharpe	1,461
1991	Michael Irvin	1,523
1990	Jerry Rice	1,502

SACKS

Year	Player	Sacks
2003	Michael Strahan	18.5
2002	Jason Taylor	18.5
2001	Michael Strahan	22.5
2000	La'Roi Glover	17.0
1999	Kevin Carter	17.0
1998	Michael Sinclair	16.5
1997	John Randle	15.5
1996	Kevin Greene	14.5
1995	Bryce Paup	17.5
1994	Kevin Greene	14.0
1993	Neil Smith	15.0
1992	Clyde Simmons	19.0
1991	Pat Swilling	17.0
1990	Derrick Thomas	20.0